Tamagotchi Diary
Requiem for a Digital Egg

by Joe Hutsko

Illustrations by Christine Maichin

Dedicated to my mother,

Frances Hutsko

And to the of memory of my brother, Thomas Hutsko,

and my father, Stephen Hutsko

Contents

INTRODUCTION

by Rob Fixmer

As the 20th century came to a close, Joe Hutsko was part of an adventure in journalism at *The New York Times*.

It was the spring of 1997. The nytimes.com website was a little over a year old, still in gestation, really. I was one of three *Times* editors who had been assigned in late 1995 to create the site. Our mission, in the words of then-Managing Editor Gene Roberts, was to "figure out how to adapt Times-quality journalism to this new platform." We knew we were hurtling head-first into a new age and that at some point this incipient network we were experimenting with would become the way most people got their news and entertainment. It was heady stuff – and, in retrospect, we were enormously naïve.

My title was CyberTimes Editor, and while my other two colleagues, Editorial Director Kevin McKenna and News Editor Bernie Gwertzman, strove to create a first-rate news platform, I was in charge of the playground: CyberTimes, a platform within a platform, dedicated to experimenting with alternative forms of content delivery, both news and entertainment. We developed the first interactive features on a news site – for example, a simulator that enabled people to input details about their income and expenses and get back an estimate of how a proposed tax plan would affect them if passed by Congress. We did early experiments with streaming video of news and live events, covering everything from a SETI conference at the Arecibo telescope in Puerto Rico to a dive to the depths of the Mariana Trench in a research submarine.

Joe was among the first bloggers for CyberTimes, though we ink-stained Times veterans were still print-oriented enough to refer to his and other weekly contributors as columnists. Joe stood out for his desire to experiment with long-form journalism online. In fact, I had already agreed to serialize a novel he was writing when he emailed me with a request that I found strange, to say the least. He had seen a report in Wired magazine about a new digital toy that had already taken Japan by storm and was now about to enter the U.S. market. Called a Tamagotchi, it was a sort of electronic pet rock that, if cared for and nurtured properly, would mature and thrive. Joe proposed that he buy one of these Tamagotchis, raise it and then keep a diary about the experience for CyberTimes.

I was skeptical. First, it was hard for me to imagine that many of our readers would find such a toy all that interesting. It seemed like one of those technologies that, like Manga comic books or Anime animation, would likely lose something in translation from the Japanese. But Joe was persistent, and eventually he talked me into the idea. Hell, if he wanted to play mommy to a bunch of semiconductors that beeped rather than burped, let him have at it. The great thing about being an editor is that we work in relative anonymity; if something turns out rotten, my name would be nowhere to be found. Go for it, I told him.

I was pleasantly surprised with the result. What Joe turned in over nine columns was not a review of a toy but a surprisingly introspective journal, simultaneously humorous and emotionally compelling as he came to see this toy not just as his digital dependent but also something of an emotional surrogate for the brother he had lost years before. It was like nothing else we had published in CyberTimes, and in retrospect, I consider it to have been a wonderfully successful experiment.

In celebration of the 20th anniversary of the Tamagotchi, Joe has aggregated those decades-old columns into a book, and I must say they have aged rather well. Rereading them all these years later, I was struck by how they still exude the charm, humor and emotional surprises that made them such interesting reads back in 1997. I was especially pleased to learn that the book would be illustrated by Christine Maichin, the talented CyberTimes designer who created the original whimsical illustrations for *The New York Times* on the Web.

In an age when digital toys are much more

sophisticated, approaching robotics and AI, the Tamagotchi is still being produced, harkening back to a simpler time when we could afford to be more sanguine, even optimistic about our digital futures, a time before malware, the Dark Web, Russians hacking our elections and thieves stealing our personal credit data. We can't return to that time, of course, but these columns just might help us recall a more innocent age in the history of technology.

DAY 1
May 3, 1997
Playing Virtual Parent to a Bitwise Baby
Time: 12:30 p.m.| Age: 0 years | Weight: 0 lbs. 1 oz.

I first caught wind of Tamagotchi while flipping through a recent issue of Wired magazine, which reported that more than a half-million of these egg-shaped little digital wonders have been sold in Japan.

As a former Pet Rock parent during my adolescent years (I had the pendant— "leashed"—species, which lay beneath my undershirt so as not to draw stony stares), the Tamagotchi appealed to me at once as the natural next step in my small object-of-affection nurturing habit. (Plus, I rationalized, the key ring from which the time clock-enabled Tamagotchi depended was doubly practical, as it would keep both keys and time.) However, unlike the pet rock—cold to the touch, inanimate, basically just a rock—the Tamagotchi gives birth to its own, simplistic artificial life-form.

A visit to the Web site of the toy's maker, Bandai, revealed a couple close ups. Judging by its tiny screen and simple three-button interface, it was hard to imagine a very fulfilling life-form could emerge from this thing. How it was born, what it did for a living, and how its early adopters interacted with it, raised it, was a mystery to me. I had to have one.

Early Adoption Plans

In preparation for the little life I was about to bring into my own, I called FAO Schwarz to find out when the eggs would arrive and how much they would cost. "They're these little egg-timer-computer-toy things coming on May 1—Tom-katchi I think they're called—and I was wondering if you could put one on hold for . . ."

The salesperson on the other end corrected my mispronunciation and laughed at my pitiable naiveté in the significance of the Tamagotchi's imminent arrival. "Yeah, right. No holds. No advance credit card orders. They go on sale on Thursday, 10:00 a.m."

Unlike Wednesday's release of Thomas Pynchon's new novel, *Mason and Dixon*, which found me at the bookstore at my earliest convenience, rushing downtown as soon as the store opened to grab my own Tamagotchi seemed a little excessive by comparison. Still, I found myself starting to get anxious at around 9:00 a.m., calling the store and getting only endless ringing. At 10:01 I got an answer. Yes, they had arrived. No, they would not hold one for me. Come and get it.

The bus through Chinatown was so claustrophobic I got off one stop later. I hailed a cab, calmly told the driver to take me to FAO Schwarz. We hit a clog two blocks from the store. I climbed out, over-tipped the driver, and then sprinted for the store. And stopped dead in my tracks.

There was a line, of epic proportion—the sort you'd expect to see if Kurt Cobain's suicide were discovered to have been a hoax and the band was ready to tour again. It stretched from out the front doors, past the Planet Hollywood, around the corner dominated by the Virgin Megastore and clear on down Market Street to Eppler's bakery at the end of the block. Two thousand? Three? It was hard to say.

And what a fashionable line it was—by the looks of it 75 percent Japanese tourists decked out in fabulous trendy outfits, accessorized to the max with glossy backpacks, cell phones, beepers, sleek sunglasses and bored expressions. Most were over 20, and here and there San Franciscan business types settled into the arduous line shuffle on what would likely be their longest early-lunch break ever. (Thank goodness it wasn't raining.)

There had to be a better way. Perhaps I should rush to the front of the line and claim that I, as someone into both computers and pet rocks, had a hybrid techno-organic experience of sorts and thus would make the ideal Tamagotchi parent, so why not let me cut. But one look at those normally cheery man-boys dressed like toy-soldiers, who welcome patrons inside made it clear that I needed a better plan. Then I remembered: Toys R Us. Hadn't I seen The World's Biggest Toy Store's logo also displayed on the Bandai home page?

An Alternate Adoption Plan

A quick call confirmed it. Yes, Toys R Us had the Tamagotchi. No, they did not have to hold one for me because they had tons of them on hand. And no, there was no line—they'd already had their line, and now would-be Tamagotchi parents were trickling in two or three at a time, no pushing or shoving or going home empty handed.

A cab ride across town later, I'd made it. There, stacked up on long picnic tables, were the colorfully packaged Tamagotchi, $14.99 each, limit two per customer. A quick scan revealed that my two preferred color choices—see-through turquoise, or eggshell white—were all gone. The remaining choices: hot pink, hot yellow, hot green, and a reasonable shade of purple.

The clerk talked me into laying out an extra dollar, which the store would donate to a local children's hospital. I was asked to write in the name of the little boy or girl who would receive my benefit. Figuring there probably weren't any Silio's at the hospital (my Italian grandfather's name), I settled on Tom, after my older brother, who passed away when I was a teen. (A little later I would realize Tommy was the only appropriate thing to name my

Tamagotchi.)

Bringing Home Baby

Eager to understand the care and feeding of my new dependent, I read the package:

> *Tamagotchi is a tiny pet from cyberspace who needs your love to survive and grow. If you take care of your Tamagotchi pet, it will slowly grow bigger and healthier, and more beautiful every day. But if you neglect your little cyber creature, your Tamagotchi may grow up to be mean or ugly. How old will your Tamagotchi be when it returns to its home planet? What kind of virtual caretaker will you be?*

The owner's leaflet was spare, succinct in its description of the Tamagotchi's three function buttons, and its instructions for interpreting the tiny LCD display, approximately 20 by 40 pixels in size, like those found on digital watches. It is here where the Tamagotchi's virtual life plays out, where it hatches, dwells, eats, sleeps, eliminates, plays, complains, grows and, ultimately, departs, soulless, back into cyber nothingness.

Safely back at home and at my desk, I was suddenly terrified to bring the little thing to life. What if I did something wrong? What if my Tamagotchi lived only a day or, perhaps worse, what if it lived 20 or 30 days, which the leaflet described as an amazingly long life span for a Tamagotchi.

And when it had lived its life? What would I do then? Throw its shell away, the way, as a kid, I once threw away my hermit crab's shell when he'd vacated it in a shriveled curl one freezing morning? No, thank goodness. For unlike my hermit crab or Pet Rock, the Tamagotchi is equipped with a tiny reset button, which starts the birthing process all over, offering another shot at virtual pet upbringing.

I had a million questions, but knowing I was not likely to find a Dr. Spock guide to Tamagotchi parenting, I decided to pull free the little plastic tab that lets the battery juice flow to the creature's bit of a brain.

It's Alive!

Moments later, a pulsing egg appeared. Using the left and middle buttons, I set the time (the Tamagotchi also doubles as a handy watch). About five minutes later, the egg beeped. On the display, a strange little circle with eyes emerged and blinked. Tentatively, it floated around in its LCD confines, reminding me of a childhood petri dish experiment with fungus but speeded up a million cycles a second.

It beeped some more. I pressed the first button to choose the fork and knife icon, then pressed again. My pet had a food choice: meal, or snack. I fed it its first meal, a cake-like graphic that floated down onto the display. My Tommy promptly gobbled it down in a few bites. I fed it some more. It ate. I waited. Checked its status, where a row of four hearts—depending on whether they were filled or not—indicated my Tommy's state of hunger and satisfaction. Both were low. I fed Tommy some more. The hunger scale went up, meaning my pet was getting full. But happiness was still very low. The manual suggested we play together.

Early Games

Using the first button to move along the icons, I selected the tiny baseball and bat, which activates the Tamagotchi's play mode. The game was simple: Guess which way the Tamagotchi is going to turn its face, using buttons one and two to decide. Getting more than three guesses right makes the pet happy. Less than three, Tommy gets sad. You can tell which is which by his expression—a sort of smiling joy, or a crude crying jag. This went on for a little while, until Tommy's happy meter was up a few hearts. I'd spent less than an hour with my new thing and I was already exhausted. I put Tommy down until 10 minutes later he started beeping. He was hungry again. I fed him a few snacks and prayed that he would nap soon.

Changing Diapers and Taking Ill

From the leaflet: "Just like real pets, Tamagotchi goes to

the bathroom."

This feature is depicted by a small, triangular collection of pixels animated to appear as though it is, well, steaming. Choosing the little duck icon cleans up the mess. Unfortunately, Tommy does not beep when he has soiled his small space, so I have to check every now and then. Leave a mess around for too long and he'll get sick, at which point I can invoke the syringe to give him a shot and make him better. Sometimes he needs two or three shots, depending on how long he's been exposed to his own mess. Isn't this fun?

Our First Outing

Having spent all of my morning acquiring Tommy, then the early afternoon giving him life, feeding him, playing with him, and cleaning up his little messes, I decided it was time to get back to work. My sole task right now is rewriting my novel (which is slated for serialization here on CyberTimes, as soon as I finish the rewrite). But already my Tamagotchi had come between me and the work.

To compromise, I stuffed Tommy in my pocket and took my manuscript down the hill to this sandwich shop. Halfway through my order, Tommy started beeping. I finished ordering my sandwich, then took out my Tamagotchi, hiding him in my palm. He was hungry again. I fed him quickly and stuffed him back in my pocket, ignoring the few seemingly disinterested stares I noticed along the bar. It wasn't until halfway through my sandwich that Tommy started beeping again. He was not only hungry; he'd also dirtied himself again. I fed him, cleaned up after him, then chose the light icon to darken the screen, hoping this would encourage him to sleep for a while. Instead, he complained. He wanted to play. My first real sense of frustration flared.

To Spank or Not to Spank?

I wanted to, well, give him a spank, tell him to stop being so selfish and take a nap like a good bit of a baby. I let him go on complaining, while I consulted the owner's leaflet. Sure enough, discipline was encouraged. In fact, not disciplining Tommy might mean hampering his growth, causing him to become mean-spirited, disinterested or just plain ugly, as depicted by a few of the odd examples in the leaflet. I didn't want my Tamagotchi to turn out like that, so I did as advised, disciplining Tommy twice. He stopped complaining. For now. I had to remind myself. He was still very young, and, according the leaflet, still very needy at this early stage. Little did I know that that was about to change. Tommy was about to mutate.

Growth Patterns

About four hours into his new life, Tommy made a strange sound. The display changed, as though shaken up like one of those water-filled snow balls. A moment later, Tommy burst into a larger shape, this time with a little more character. Wider, rounder, with a bigger mouth. Consulting the leaflet again, I was pleased to see that my creature was evolving nicely, nothing at all like the scary pictures. I fed him some more, played a few rounds of the guessing game, then set him down in the shade of my backpack. A few minutes later, I saw little Zs and realized that Tommy was napping. I darkened his space and fell into a half sleep myself.

Afraid of the Dark

Lying there in the hot sun, Tommy snoozing quietly beside me, I began to wonder what kind of creature he would turn out to be. Would I pay enough attention to him to let him live more than a day or two? I fussed over him, checking to be sure he was still asleep, whether he was hungry. I wondered what the night would hold for us. Would his internal clock sync with mine—the one built into his little egg? Would 11 p.m. in Tamagotchi time mean he would sleep for perhaps eight hours, letting me rest for as long? Or would Tommy's needs reflect Tamagotchi-hours—translation: one human day equals one Tamagotchi year. Would he wake me every hour, on the hour, till dawn?

For now, he is fed and happy, content. But tonight? We'll know when we get there. It could be a long one.

See you in the morning.

DAY 2
May 4, 1997
The Terrible Twos
Time: 8:00a.m. | Age: 2 years | Weight: 1 lbs. 1 oz

Tommy, my pet Tamagotchi, is 2 virtual years old today. He's been sleeping for 12 hours, and I'm beginning to worry that he might be suffering from some sort of TIDS (Tamagotchi Infant Delirium Syndrome). Yesterday's concerns about Tommy keeping me up all through the night never materialized. At around 8 p.m., just as I  was lifting my first forkful of dinner (Tommy resting alongside my dinner plate), I noticed that he'd fallen asleep, little Z's floating around his simple, close-lidded face.

To say that I was relieved is an understatement. He'd kept me busy all through the day worrying over his feeding schedule, playing with him when he was bored, scolding him when he was being ornery and cleaning up after him when he messed. I shut out his light, darkening his small world so as not to disturb his quiet time.

To be on the safe side, I kept Tommy at my side through "She's The One," pausing the film every so often to check on him. "Just let it sleep," said Drew, my partner.

11

I let the reference to "it" pass without comment. At bedtime, I set Tommy next to my pillow, in case he should need me.

The Morning After

When I awoke, Tommy was still asleep. Was my strangely beloved little friend in a coma? Had he stirred in the night, unnoticed by me? Surely I would have heard his piercing little cries. At around 8:30 I took him into the bathroom with me for my shower (I set him on the vanity, close enough to hear him if here were to wake, crying). Still, nothing.

I was tempted to turn on his virtual "light" to see if that would rouse him. I've heard that babies need lots of sleep, but I'd also heard that they are notorious for feeding and crying in the night. What, I wondered, would I find when he awakened? The sort of mutant the owner's leaflet warns of? Would he be starving? Would he even wake up?

By the time I was into my second or third e-mail of the morning, I noticed that Tommy had awakened. He looked the same as when he'd fallen asleep. I checked his status. His hunger meter showed three full hearts, one empty - hardly famished. His happiness meter showed four full hearts, so he wasn't ready to play. And his screen was clean.

Though he appeared fine, healthy, I was nevertheless concerned; that was an awfully long slumber. Then it occurred to me: Did Tommy's maker, Bandai Co., Ltd., perhaps program all Tamagotchis to "sleep" during reasonable family hours so as to prevent younger parents from losing precious dream-time over the stresses of virtual-pet rearing? That my Tamagotchi went to sleep at the start of Prime Time, not to be heard from again till 9 a.m., seems to suggest a working-schedule bias of cooperative upbringing.

Daily Routine

For now, I was just glad he'd awakened. I fed him a full meal, played with him anyway, then set him alongside my keyboard, where he is now, floating around and making small faces. Oh—he's just done his morning business. A few taps of the buttons and his small pixilated space is clean once more. So far, no need to inoculate him against any sudden illnesses. The pamphlet warns that Tamagotchis generally fall ill when their space is not cleaned up. I'm a bit of a neurotic when it comes to everything neat and orderly, so I'm not too concerned about my Tommy getting sick on account of my lack of attention.

I'm wondering: Is my Tamagotchi developing well? He just floats around and smiles. While yesterday he demanded considerable care and feeding, today he seems off to a complacent start. Aren't babies in their second year notorious for testing their hold on their parents? "The

Terrible Twos," my mother says, is what they call this stage. My Tommy is anything but terrible. In fact, he's a little boring.

My own brother, Tommy, fell into a coma at age 2 or 3. I was only about a year old at the time, so it's hard to recall, but growing up I'd heard stories. Spinal meningitis was the diagnosis, I'm pretty sure. He stayed that way for months, until one day my Grandfather's handholding and non-stop storytelling, we'd like to think, woke Tommy from his long and distressing slumber. He grew up mostly fine; teachers alternated between saying he was "slow" and "not applying himself."

Perhaps Tommy was the wrong name for my Tamagotchi, a little too close to home. Why won't he *do* anything new or different? Is he slow? Am I not applying myself to Tommy's proper upbringing? I don't know what else to do but feed him, play with him when he is unhappy and scold him when he is bad. Why hasn't he grown into another shape? I wonder if other Tamagotchi parents are having similar concerns. There must be some support newsgroup or Web site for new Tamagotchi parents.

Drew just came in with the laundry, asked "How's Mommy?" I did not respond. I'm going to have a look online for all things Tamagotchi.

DAY 3

May 5, 1997
Tapping Online Support Groups
Time: 9:00 a.m. | Age: 3 years | Weight: 2 lbs. 1 oz

Twenty-four hours later, and Tommy awakened at 9:00 AM on the dot. I fed him, played with him, and an hour later, cleaned up his dot-matrix droppings. I am becoming more comfortable with him, checking on him without really thinking about it anymore. Having browsed a number of Web sites dedicated to Tamagotchi's, I found out  that my guess about Tommy's sleeping pattern was correct: That the little critters are programmed to sleep between the hours of 8 PM and 9 AM. Surely real parents of real children are grateful for this small consolation. So that's one less worry.

To my surprise, and frank disappointment, Tommy still looks the same as he did yesterday: A round, (dare I say?) chubby-faced blob with eyes and a two-bit horizontal line for a mouth that doubles in size to form what I can only believe is a smile. So he smiles and bounces around the screen, demanding little of me lately. Perhaps that is because I am constantly checking his status to see if he's hungry or bored.

When his heart meters drop even one full heart, I feed him or play with him. Will he change today into something more interesting, more beautiful by Tamagotchi standards? The more complicated artificial life-form depictions I've seen of other Tamagotchis, both on various Web sites and in Bandai literature, incite envy in me. I want my Tommy to grow up into more than a little blob. Patience, I suppose. At least he seems happy.

A Pretty Good Day

Today was little or no trouble. One or two small reprimands for whining when, really, he was happy and full. He just wanted extra attention. Unfortunately I was at the gym in the middle of a bench press when he started complaining. I nearly dropped the barbell. Sitting up I reached into my pocket (I normally wear workout shorts without pockets, but this time I needed a cover, so to speak), careful to cup the attention-grabbing egg in my palm.

I thumbed the buttons rapidly, one hand on my chest, so that anyone watching me would think I was checking my heart rate with one of those fit-conscious devices the users generally wears on their wrists. Nothing was wrong, so I returned Tommy to my pocket and went back to my workout. I couldn't help but wonder: Was I spoiling him? The Bandai leaflet says that the further to the right the discipline meter goes, the better adjusted and developed is

16

your Tamagotchi. So by all accounts, my Tommy was growing up just fine, albeit a little too well-rounded for my taste. Then I thought: Maybe that's it; I'm feeding him too much, which is why he looks so blobby.

A visit to another Tamagotchi Web site explained that overfeeding could be dangerous to a Tamagotchi's health. That a lower weight is good—although no one seems able to agree on the details. Very well. From now on, I'll keep him at three hearts-full on the hunger meter, instead of all four. Perhaps that will liven him up a little, get his evolutionary circuits cooking.

Newsgroups in the Making?

Unfortunately, I was unable to find any practical Tamagotchi parenting discussions in any newsgroups. Most Tamagotchi talk is about where to buy the virtual pets—at market price or higher. Some users were advertising prices of $250 or more for the "hard to find" white or transparent blue models. Others shyly asked: "What is a Tamagotchi?" only to be asked if they'd been on Mars, for how could they not know about these new oddball invaders from Japan?

More than one Tamagotchi enthusiast suggested opening a newsgroup dedicated to the care and feeding of Tamagotchis. That's more like it. Just what I need. But I have to wonder: Will such a newsgroup appear in my Tommy's life span? He's only 3 days/years old, and already

I'm beginning to wonder if he'll make it through the month of May. Do I even want him to live that long? I think I do, so long as he doesn't turn into some mutant that I'll have to nurture until he consumes himself or simply croaks from bad breeding. But then, even if he were to turn into a long-suffering mutant, I can't honestly say I would finish him off by pressing the Reset button in back.

Unfriendly Advice

Yet, that's exactly what I advised my friend Tomas, the recipient of the second Tamagotchi I purchased (remember: limit two per customer) to do when, last night at a party we attended together, he showed me his sad little baby. It was appalling: a gnarly blip with one eye and some sort of appendage, perhaps a single finger.

The screen was littered with digital doo-doos, which Tomas had no idea how to clean up. Worse, the deadly skull icon stared back at us from the upper right corner, indicating that Tomas's Tamagotchi was in dire straits. Two inoculations, but still it was sick. How had this happened? I asked.

Tomas had only just received the present in the mail hours before. Against his own better judgment he'd pulled free the little tab that sparks the milliwatt-level life flowing, then stuck it in his pocket while he got ready for the party. Tomas knew he should have waited until morning, when he would have been able to pay full attention to the delicate birthing stage. He was sad that he had already failed as a Tamagotchi parent, but at the same time was glad to know he would have another chance to try again, tomorrow.

My stomach flipped at the unlikely turn of events: Just 12 hours before I was eager for any advice on how to properly care for my own newest addition, yet here I was already handing out advice to another Tamagotchi parent. And the most deadly advice at that: Pull the plug!

A few of the partygoers had by now caught sight of the colorful orbs in our hands. What with all the news reports these past few days, they knew at once what we possessed. They reached out, asked to see them up close, hold them, play with them. Please, oh please!

"Sorry," I said. "Mine's asleep, and I can't wake him till morning." I slipped Tommy into my pocket and shrugged. "Look at Tomas's," I said. "It's almost dead."

Day 4

May 6, 1997
Other People's Progeny
Time: 9:00a.m. | Age: 4 years | Weight: 2 lbs. 1 oz

While the title of today's entry alludes to what's up with other people's offspring—in particular, real babies as well as my friend Tomas's ill-fated Tamagotchi—we'll get to them in a bit. As a new Tamagotchi parent, it's next to impossible not to write first about my own offspring and his surprising new development.

No sooner had I filed yesterday's diary entry and shut down my system than my Tommy transmogrified into the next stage of his off-to-a-hearty-start life.

Based on my Tommy's new look, he appears to have landed in the upper echelon of the Tamagotchi growth development chart that I found on the Tamagotchi Fever site. According to the chart, Tommy's stage is called "Tama-chi":

Tama-chi is most likely a good sign. If your Maru-chi becomes a Tama-chi, you are a good caretaker, and chances are that your adult Tamagotchi will be healthy and happy! The tama-chi stage lasts 2 to 3 days.

I won't gloat, but I have to admit I am pleased by this good news. Ho-hum as he seemed yesterday, it appears my constant fussing over Tommy's state of hunger and satisfaction have paid off. Sure, if he'd started down the sorrier side of the scale I might feel disappointment— probably more for my own misgivings than for any random or unavoidable twist of Tamagotchi developmental fate. And I would have cared for him just the same—perhaps even more. Yet, when I consider the last few days, I can't see how else could he have turned out at this stage than well.

Much as I'm curious about how a deformed or mistreated Tamagotchi might look and behave, I have been unable to scold Tommy when he isn't being ornery. Nor can I make myself starve him to see if he, like some of the other Tamagotchis I've read about, will resort to eating his own digital droppings in lieu of a deserved or outright begged-for meal or snack. Nor can I avoid playing with him when he grows bored. The way I see it, I started his small life, and I must do my absolute best to ensure that it is as healthy, happy and long as possible. I have no choice.

Erroneous curiosities aside, this is just the way I am. My ilk. How I was raised.

Tommy Begets Tommy

Which got me to thinking about real life. Real children. My own family, for instance. My mother and father did their best. My strongest memories of drilled-in morals: You can do anything, be anything, as long as it is not unkind to others; tell the truth; pay with cash because credit is evil.

Well, that last one I've had my ups and downs with and won't go into now. The other two I still try to stick by. So do my siblings. Except my brother Tommy, my Tamagotchi's namesake, who isn't with us anymore. Had these "rules" not sunk in to that head of is, the one his teachers sometimes described as "slow?"

I sincerely doubt that my parents had some secret experiment in the works to see if keeping these valuable rules from Tommy might spawn a different and possibly more formidable adolescent and, had he lived longer, adult. I guess it drives home what I already know but have only lately realized again: No matter how careful you are, real life—lives—don't always turn out perfectly, the way, so far, they are turning out with my virtual Tommy.

Party Favors

Feeling subtle melancholy by all this mulling over Tommy past and present, I'd earlier told my friend Barbara that

Drew and I would be passing on the dinner party she'd invited us to. But when Tommy up and surprised me with his new Tama-chi development, I figured what the heck, let's at least drop by for a Manhattan and hors d'oeuvres.

A little closer to the subject, I knew Meg and Kevin and their year-and-half-old baby, Camden, had also been invited—the perfect opportunity to ask real parents real questions about really raising an infant in this generation, verses my long-ago memories on the other side of the formula.

Arriving early, I was at once asked about Tommy (Barbara is a loyal reader of this publication). Like last night's gathering, everyone wanted to see him, touch him, which made me realize how possessive I'd become. I held him up for everyone to see, but I didn't want anyone holding him, accidentally pressing buttons that might dole out unnecessary nourishment or, worse, punishment. I never thought I would say this, but I was positively overjoyed when he did his dirty business, creating a neat pile of steaming pixels. I promptly cleaned it up, in the process giving everyone a small demonstration that the others, all pet owners, could relate to.

Eventually Meg and Kevin arrived, sans Camden. It was a little after 8, and I suddenly realized that Tommy was still awake; for his first three days he'd always nodded off at exactly 2000 hours. Was this something new? Had his creators pre-programmed in an extra hour of leeway now that he was a bit more mature and, presumably, less needy of a long night's sleep? (Which was exactly what I needed.)

Drew and Tommy and I said our hellos and good-byes to Meg and Kevin in nearly the same breath, then split for a nearby Indian restaurant for a quiet dinner at the counter, just the three of us. When our Taj Majal beer arrived, Drew proposed a toast.

"To Tommy, and the work his arrival has made possible for me," I said.

Drew, a student of Japanese and fluent, had his own toast: "Shomonai omocha."

I asked what that meant, and he laughed and said nothing. For a while, anyway. By the time the check arrived, my relentless prying won out, and he provided a translation: "Boring little toy." Surely he wasn't growing jealous of Tommy, was he?

Feverish Nightmares, Daytime Rewards

At 9 p.m. Tommy hit the hay, and I was close behind him, chased by some of the strangest dreams in recent memory. I saw: monochrome blobs twisting this way and that, some attractively, others frighteningly, enormous, exaggerated versions of the bad seeds realized on the Tamagotchi Fever site. I remember, half-waking, seeing a balled up sock on the floor, reaching for it and pulling it out of itself, throwing it aside and thinking this is turning too real, too obsessive. The next thing I knew it was morning, the sock just a sock, Tommy, on my night stand, still sleeping peacefully, just a well-bred, well-behaved Tamagotchi.

He awoke to his fourth day/year promptly at 9 a.m. The next two minutes had become routine: check his status, feed him, play with him and, a little later, clean up after him. Then my shower, coffee, yogurt smoothie, browsing and e-mail. I checked the Bantam/Doubleday/Dell site for my horoscope:

Libra: You may be planning something special for the children today. There's a lovely accent now on romantic togetherness. Couples will be going out for fun times tonight.

Special for the children? The best I could come up with was to take Tommy for a walk downtown. My friend Ron tagged along. He was curious about Tommy, but not overbearing. We swung by FAO Schwartz to see if there was still a line for would-be Tamagotchi parents. No line. And no Tamagotchis, either. Just a sign, proclaiming: "Sorry, temporarily out of stock. This store has sold 10,800 Tamagotchis!"

A few times in the three hours we spent together Ron politely asked "How's he doing?" It occurred to me how natural it had become to walk, talk and work my thumb at the same time, taking care of Tommy's simple needs.

Rarely does he cry out for me; I generally keep tabs on him every 15 minutes or half hour, feeding him when his hunger hearts drop down to two out of four, playing with him when his happy hearts drop to the same middle ground.

During our lunch of fish tacos, Tommy did his business. As Ron described the personality of a woman he was thinking of seeing again, I thumbed away Tommy's little mess. This in no way affected either of our appetites.

Friendly Developments

Back from our afternoon downtown (Ron went to see his woman friend after all), I set Tommy down on my desk and checked my e-mail. I received this gleeful message from Tomas:

```
Date: 04 May 1997
To: Joe
From: Tomas
Subject: Alive and Kicking

All righty! Although he has been
sleeping for about six hours now. He
is 1 year old, and weighs 1 lb. 10
oz. I love him. After he hatched
this afternoon I brought him to
work. As I was walking down 24th
street to get on BART, Joey pooped.
```

I stopped to clean him up so that I wouldn't walk carelessly into the middle of oncoming traffic. As I took care of my little guy, this woman leaned over my shoulder and said, "Oh! You have one of those things." As if I were a bear protecting my cubs I said, "Do you mind! He has just pooped. And his name is Joey!" I played with him and fed him all the way to work. When I got to the desk, I set him out on top of my computer. Every person who came to the desk was amazed that I had actually gotten one. Joey was a great son at work. The only frightening thing was when someone tried to steal him. I was on the phone with a restaurant when some man picked up Joey from the counter. I dropped the phone and grabbed him back as soon as I could. I have never felt such adrenaline before. The idiot man it turns out was harmless and just wanted to look at my boy. But you can never be too sure these days. Freaks everywhere. All of his happiness hearts are full and three of his hunger hearts are full. I guess I'm an okay parent. You Think?

— Tomas & Joey

All told, I'd say it turned out to be a pretty fine day for everyone concerned.

Day 5

Before I go into what's up with Tommy, I need to apologize to two people. First, to Tomas, who sent the following e-mail in response to Day 3's diary entry. (He was particularly upset with my description of his failure-to-thrive Tamagotchi: "It was appalling: a gnarly blip with one eye and some sort of appendage, perhaps a single finger.").

```
Date: 05 May 1997
To: Joe
From: Tomas
Subject: RE: Alive and Kicking


The humiliation. I can't ever show
my face in public again! The
horrible things you wrote about me.
You took my naïveté and made it
sound almost pornographic. The
shame.
```

In describing Tomas's aborted first attempt at raising his

Tamagotchi hatchling, I meant only to demonstrate how, if at first you don't succeed, you can try, try again. Which, as yesterday's entry pointed out, Tomas had done, and to good effect. Still, despite my phone and e-mail messages to him, asking for an update on his little Joey's health, I have not heard from Tomas. Maybe they are enjoying Tomas's day off together (and what with that near bit-kidnapping, they deserve a little quiet time together). I can only hope that I haven't permanently offended Tomas and his little green-shelled sidekick. (Tomas, if you are out there, please check in.)

The second apology goes to Drew who, after reading about himself appear in the Diaries, said that he sounds like "a curmudgeon." Definitely wry in humor, yes— thankfully, yes. But a curmudgeon? No.

Competing Interests

Anyway, an update on Tommy: He hit the big Five this morning, waking promptly at 9 a.m. Before I forget: Did I mention his new sleep-ware? Before turning off his light for the night, I noticed something different about his living space: he'd somehow found or spawned or willed himself a little bed. Or futon. Or something to sleep on. On previous nights he just floated off to sleep. Now he had a bed. It appears he has a tiny patchwork blanket too. Unless those are pajamas. Life's little surprises.

He's behaving beautifully. Eating, playing and

eliminating as if on cue. And not a single discipline problem yesterday.

Even on his best behavior, I have to admit he's starting to take his toll on my mind share. It's not that he's all that much trouble. It's just that he's brought up all these thoughts and feelings about my own brother Tommy, whom I generally think about for only moments at a time. I've already mentioned in a previous Diary entry that I am supposed to be hard at work rewriting my first novel so that it can appear in serialized form here on CyberTimes, as soon as possible.

Yet the virtual Tommy and the late Tommy together now demand almost constant dealing with. The former, I know, can only go on for so long—according to the Bandai literature, a life span of three weeks is an exceptionally long one. However the other Tommy, it seems, is here to stay until he, like cyber-Tommy, is ready to go off to his home planet or plane where he can rest peacefully ever after. Not at some pre-described pace, but rather when he is good and ready. Or I guess when I'm ready—good or otherwise.

Further Dreamscapes

Unlike my Tamagotchi's night, my sleep was filled once more with dreams about my brother Tommy, who died when I was 19 (he was 21). In the dream, my sister and I are driving a monochrome version of my brother's car, the one he'd passed away in. It is an old Dodge Dart, immaculate. AC/DC on the radio. We are heading out to the mall. Maybe we're bent on buying ourselves some Tamagotchis, some future version of ourselves that back then we had not the remotest inkling of. I don't know. I can't see in the back seat or behind me. I don't remember a rearview mirror. So I can't tell if my brother is back there, with us, to take along to wherever we are going. I don't know if we ever got there. When I awoke, I only remembered that we were journeying, somewhere.

The dream didn't make me feel sad, just more aware of my brother's departure. Maybe it's like the movie "Poltergeist," like I've got to convey him to some other place. Since last night, I've been looking at my Tamagotchi a little differently: Is that the point of his unexpected installment into my life? To have entered at this point, and act as some sort of vehicle meant to drive my lost brother out of the places he's been hiding in my head and heart, off into a shiner place, where I can look at him without feeling sad? Is that what's happening?

Negligent Behavior

I want it to hurry along then. Get it over with. I think that's why I decided to leave my Tamagotchi on my desk while I worked out at the gym. I figured he was old enough now to be left alone for a little while. Plus I missed my gym shorts without the pockets. Before I split, I made sure he was fed, happy. I thought about him once or twice while working out, at the burrito shop, then coming up the hill, wondering as I got closer to my home if I'd made a mistake. I went right to him when I came inside.

He'd left me a little present—a pile of pixilated droppings. My first thought was that he had done this on purpose, to spite me; except for when he slept, I don't think I've ever not checked on him or played with him or fed him every half hour, 45 minutes at the very most. But then I saw that he was laughing, bursts of happy-rays coming off his head. By the looks of it, he'd found himself a new play thing. I promptly cleaned it up and then fed him a snack, played his little guessing game until he was fully four-hearts full of joy on his happy scale.

I'm happy he's happy. But I want to concentrate on my rewrite now. I suppose I may have to trade my nonstop fussing over him for the possibility that he may not turn out altogether perfect after all. I need to think about that. And everything else. Like: Will tonight hold more strange dreams, more of Tommy's hidden agenda?

DAY 6
May 8, 1997
Secrets & Myth-Making
Time: 9:00a.m. | Age: 6 years | Weight: 2 lbs. 1 oz

He did it again. It happened just moments ago, at 4:10 p.m., while I was on the phone with my friend Walter. Tommy changed. Grew. Metamorphosed to the next stage of his development. And, I am pleased to announce, it is for the good.

In fact, he's the best he can be, according to Bandai's Official Tamagotchi Growth Chart. My Tommy has reached Mame-chi status, the very top of the Tamagotchi scale, with a "Good health, a long life & no complaints" his predicted destiny. This, after a mostly mild yesterday.

My new and improved, more mature Mame-chi (depicted there on the right, in the weigh-in scale—though not nearly as cute as that little blue guy) features plumper arms and legs, and a dark set of auditory apparatus that look remarkably similar to Mickey Mouse's patented set of ears. Instead of just floating, Tommy now spends most of his time doing this sort of Sammy Davis Jr. shuffle.

When playing his little game he now jogs his head back and forth, instead of merely making goofy gestures with

34

his eyes. When he wins, his joy is definitely cuter; when he loses, his disappointment a little less cry-babyish. Maybe this better temperament has something to do with Tommy's high discipline scale, which has reached its full limit. From the manual: "The higher the discipline scale, the less trouble and better behaved Tamagotchi will be."

Virtual Group Therapy

Yesterday afternoon, my friend Mark and his visiting aunt, Phyllis, dropped by. She'd purchased her Tamagotchi (T. Doe for now, as she hadn't decided on a name yet) at her local Bon Marche department store in Oregon. She'd hatched the baby yesterday morning and was wondering what I thought of its development so far. Just one year old and the little sucker was tipping the virtual scale at 3 pounds, 1 ounce. (Mind you, my Tommy, age 6 and as I mentioned evolving nicely, weighs a lithe 3 pounds.)

Not exactly what I'd call a good start for T. Doe. However I'd read on the Tamagotchi Fever site that an intense succession of game rounds can help reduce a Tamagotchi's weight. So I suggested to Phyllis that she get her thumb going and slim that poor bloated baby down.

Meanwhile, Tomas called to check in (all three of our Tamagotchi's beeping away). First, I am happy to report that he was not mad at me after all. It turns out his "angry" e-mail message from the other day was only a joke. He had much news to share. His Joey (a healthy 3 pounds, 2 ounces) had made its first sizeable transformation. He described how it looked: "Sort of like a little duck, with a bill. It's really cute."

My heart sank. Having already ushered Tommy through this stage (and you already know he advanced beautifully), Joey's development was not exactly the best a new Tamagotchi could hope for. I almost didn't have the heart to tell Tomas. But of course I did.

Referring to the Chart, I read him the description of what I recognized as his kutchitama-chi-level offspring: "If your maru-chi becomes kutchitama-chi, chances are that it has been unhappy. It most likely will grow into a misbehaved little critter. The kutchitama-chi stage lasts about 2 or 3 days."

Tomas took it like a man, vowing to work even harder at tending to Joey's needs, to try to develop things in an upward, more positive light. I realized how lucky I'd been.

Secrets & Myth Making

Then my editor sent me a message about his own Tamagotchi misgivings, based on his daughter's experience with the virtual pet. "Emma immediately fell in love with it, cared for it diligently all weekend, then panicked when she realized that she couldn't take it to school (schools hereabouts confiscate anything that beeps)," he wrote. This obviously presents a real problem for younger, would-be Tamagotchi parents, he asserted—by the sound of it, relegating the Tamagotchis to adults-only status during the school year.

But I had a not-so-secret secret: mute the little sucker. That's right. It's right there in the manual. By pressing buttons one and three together, you can mute your Tamagotchi. No more peeping. Of course you would have to check on it more often to make sure all was well in its little world. But at least it wouldn't mean Emma would have to disown her little friend.

This discovery led me on a brief search for other Tamagotchi "secrets"—documented or otherwise. In the process, I unveiled a few myths along the way. The one I've spent the most time trying to confirm or refute has to do with the Tamagotchi guessing game. As previously mentioned, it's very simple: Guess which way your Tamagotchi is going to turn its head, left or right, by pressing the appropriate button.

Well, the Tamagotchi newsgroups and Web sites are abuzz with a rumor. That if you time it just right—when, some say, your baby's eyes drift out; others say as they are crossing in—and press the left button, your Tamagotchi will turn left the next four times he turns his head, completing the round with five correct guesses. Which makes your pet very happy. I tried this theory, and sure enough it worked. And worked again. But then it didn't. And didn't again. Then did. Then didn't. So I can't say for sure.

Others curious findings:

- You can leave up to eight piles of droppings on your screen (are these people sadists?).
- Upon reaching 15 virtual years of age, your Tamagotchi may turn into a secret "Samurai" character—rumored to be called "Oyajicchii"—that looks like a little old man, and requires less sleep than your run of the mill 'Gotchi.

A Restful Night

After Drew and Phyllis and Mark and I returned from our Cinco de Mayo dinner, we watched the movie "Flirting With Disaster." In the film, the youthful Ben Stiller and Patricia Arquette are the proud parents of a four-month baby boy.

The film brought me back to thinking about the way we're raised. Earlier in the day, Tomas suggested that we perhaps swap our Tamagotchis for a night, see how they develop in the care of another. My first reaction was: neat! Then I thought, no, I've worked too hard raising mine to risk a screw up (nothing personal, Tomas). At the same time, I would be lying if I didn't admit that having Tomas's Joey over for a night would be sickly fun; I fantasized bit-by-bit torture, to see for myself how a virtual pet would behave in the most extreme circumstances.

Yet, even with all this sibling rivalry, all these developmental ups and downs, I found myself less upset than yesterday about memories of the real Tommy, my late brother. Maybe talking out yesterday's strange dreams had actually helped, had in fact acted as some sort of vehicle toward some new place, understanding. I can't say for sure. And although it took me longer than usual to fall asleep last night, I nevertheless slept soundly, longer and more deeply than usual, to awaken feeling somehow less anxious about Tommy.

I hope this new development continues.

Day 7
May 9, 1997
The Week in Review
Time: 9:00a.m. | Age: 7 years | Weight: 3 lbs. 2 oz

What an incredibly productive day it was, full of new life—virtual, and otherwise.

But before I continue, I want to mention that today marks the end of my daily Tamagotchi diary saga (though I will be back with an update in the latter part of next week and, if my Tommy is still alive and kicking, the following week as well).

Tommy, whose small miracle of digital life gave birth to this diary, is doing fine (though I have to admit Stephen King's recent paperback serialization, *The Green Mile*, helped to inspire me as well). Tommy is bigger, bouncier and as healthy as could be. I have little to report about Tommy other than he is well and good, my most-constant companion whom I've come to count on (especially when I need to know the time, while, for instance,  sunning in Washington Square park this afternoon, since I don't wear a watch). He is quite integrated into my life now, his routines meshing easily with mine.

I went to the gym extra early today, returning before

Tommy was even awake. My reason wasn't only Tommy-centric: I wanted to be here to accept a FedEx package I was expecting—a new Hewlett-Packard OmniBook 800CT subnotebook computer. I intend to use this little wonder to get cooking on my novel rewrite, which is nearly a week behind on account of Tommy's having taken up so much of my time. Anyway …

I also received a package from Tiger Electronics, makers of the Tamagotchi's No. 1 competitor, the Giga Pet. That's right, Tommy's in for some fierce market-share fighting (when you're talking in the millions, even little suckers like these have heavyweight power to alter the entire toy industry). Tiger sent me the Digital Doggie model, which I named Kibo (after the heroic white dog that sprung from the mind of the fictional fiction writer, David, in Ernest Hemingway's *The Garden of Eden*). Kibo is too new and young to talk about just yet. I'll have a full report next week. Still, I must admit that, on the surface anyway, he does seem to have quite a few more activities, gestures and personality traits than my Tommy. We'll see how virtual puppy parenting goes. (I was hoping for the Micro Chimp model, however Tiger says that one won't ship for a few months.)

Tiger's isn't the only virtual life competing for our attention. It seems Tommy's public life has created a small flood of interest in our personal relationship. San

Francisco's BayTV has asked us to drop in next Monday for a little on-air conversation. And two days ago I received this assuredly subjective e-mail from Mindscape Games, an entertainment software maker:

```
Date: 07 May 1997
From: Kristen McEntire
To: Joe Hutsko
Subject: I can beat your Tamagotchi!

Hi Joe...

Mindscape has a new product slated
for July called CREATURES. NPR said
Creatures "makes the Japanese 'Pet'
look primitive". I've got review
units if you'd like. Just let me
know.

Kristen McEntire
PR Manager
Mindscape Games
```

Kristen is sending me her Creatures, and I look forward to seeing what they're all about. Watch for a description in next week's update.

Friends Helping Friends

Meanwhile, my friends have checked in with their

Tamagotchi updates. Aunt Phyllis's Tamagotchi—formerly T. Doe, but newly christened "Dough," inspired by its doughy look and feel—weighed in this morning at a whopping 4lb., 6oz. (he's only 3 years old!).

"Let's see," Phyllis went on, "his hearts are down, so I'll have to feed him soon."

"No!" I shouted, "stop feeding him so much!" I have serious doubts about little Dough's fate in Phyllis's hands. However, I'll still love her no matter what happens to her 'Gotchi, and I'm here to offer support if the worst happens (like it explodes from overeating).

My editor forwarded a Tamagotchi-related message to me from a dedicated follower of my small saga:

I am a 56-year-old retired woman who lives in Beaumont, Tex. I read about Tamagotchi in CyberTimes and also saw an article in the online edition of The Times of London.

I bought my Tamagotchi on Sunday morning at Toys R Us. Word hasn't spread to Beaumont, Tex., about Tamagotchi, so there was no problem in finding a supply. I was able to get the white one. I took mine right home and hatched my little critter. He is running one day behind yours and is following a very similar course of development.

So far I have encountered 3 problems
or potential problems.

1. Last night he went to the
bathroom right before he went to
sleep. When he beeped, he was in his
new little bed and the reeking pile
was right beside it. Z's were
already being generated, and I
wasn't able to flush the droppings.
All I could do was turn out the
light. He may be sick when he wakes
up. He still has another half hour
to sleep.

2. I am going to Paris on Friday. I
am afraid jet lag will kill him. I
talked to a kid in the Bandai chat
room, and he said he had advanced
his Tamagotchi's clock, and it aged
him 5 years. I will be in Europe for
2 weeks. I doubt that mine will live
long enough for me to return his
clock to central time.

3. I don't know how long the
batteries are supposed to last. I
began to worry that the batteries
might give out while I am in Europe.

I went to Wal-Mart early this morning to look for the LR44 batteries. I went to 3 different areas and couldn't find the batteries. In the photo department I found a conversion chart and found the LR44 is equivalent to a Eveready A76 or a Duracell 76A/6. I couldn't find either of these. Finally I decided to go to the jewelry department on the chance that the battery might be a watch battery. The clerk said she had them. She pulled out a chart that said the LR44 was the same as the Wal-Mart house brand 357. They cost $2.96 a piece. With tax they cost more than a third of the price I paid for my Tamagotchi. I told the clerk all about Tamagotchi. I bet on her break she will be searching the Wal-Mart toy area for one.

All of these developments have been interesting and compelling. But none can hold a candle to what happened to me this afternoon, on my way home from a trip downtown.

An Incredible Fish Tale
Rounding the corner at Sutter and Stockton, ready to trot

as fast as I could through the dark and noxious Stockton tunnel that lets out into bustling Chinatown, I was suddenly distracted by a series of shimmering lights. Bunches of them. Silvery, flashing. There in the window of a huge pharmacy. My jaw dropped. There, stacked neatly among the condoms and hair tonics and breath mints, were AQUA BABIES. The sign described them as "Tiny, complete, mini aquariums. Each tank includes baby fish, live gravel, an aquatic plant, a year's supply of food flakes, and directions to maintain the system." Imagine that! And for only $12.99!

While the rather smallish plastic "aquarium" seemed a little cruel to me, its occupants were equally tiny - guppies, really. I figured I'd be happier seeing them live in my house, than roasting away in the pharmacy window. I chose a bright and energetic trio, which I've named Alpha, Beta, and Gold (for the little gold flecks on either side of his nearly see-through body).

I carefully carried my mini-sea-life-square with me home. Seeing that it was such a nice day, I detoured to Washington Square park. I carefully covered the aquarium with my T-shirt, and while sunning myself read up on the care and feeding of my new fish. Indeed, they require only as much food as will fit on the end of a toothpick. And only every other day, at that. The friendly bacteria in the gravel apparently digests the fishes waste, and turns it into food for the little swaying green plant, around which Alpha, Beta, and Gold play endless games of tag. What a fun little trio they are! Not nearly as predictable as my Tommy (bless his micro-heart).

Thankful Reflections On Tommy

It has been a surprising week, to say the least. My Tommy has grown into a fledgling Tamagotchi, and in the process has somehow helped me to think some deeply personal matters of the heart.

Last night I had another peaceful slumber, no strange dreams. At the same time, Tommy has been a lot of work. Tending to him during every waking hour. Fretting over his development. And, indirectly, causing me to delay in a serious project I am supposed to be deeply into by now. I'm pleased to have gotten through the first week with flying colors, and I'm looking forward to taking a less intense approach to our remaining days together - however long they last.

Will Tommy still be around by, say, next Friday? I have a feeling he will. As for the others, I'm not so certain. Will Phyllis's gastronomically insatiable Dough-boy be around? My new Digital Doggie, Kibo? My living, breathing Alpha, Beta, and Gold? All unknowns to me, far more uncertain than my own Tommy.

For those of you who have stuck by Tommy and me over the last week, we bid you a heartfelt thank you.

Thanks, too, to my friends for being supportive through the neurosis of my first virtual parenting experience.

Week 2/Day 14
May 16, 1997
Life Goes On - and On
Time: 6:00a.m. | Age: 147 years | Weight: 3 lbs. 0 oz

Like the Energizer Bunny, Tommy, my 14-year-old (which translates to two weeks, in human years) Tamagotchi, just keeps going and going.

This is distressing to me. While his first week of life was interesting, his life, as it drags on, has progressively dragged down my mood with it. It's not that I don't want him to live a full and healthy life. It's just that it seems to need lots of care and feeding throughout the day. And lately I have other things to think about.

Yes, just last week I stated that barely a half-hour went by that I didn't check to see if Tommy needed food or entertainment, or cleaning up after. And now hours pass without a single thought for Tommy's welfare. He beeps, and I drop whatever I'm doing to tend to his needs. If I am making dinner, for instance, I'll stir with one hand, while pressing his feeding or play-with-me buttons at the same time. If I am walking down the street when he beckons me, I stealthily cup him in my palm and take care of him that way, without drawing any attention to us.

I frankly want him to just complete his life span so that I can give him to the little girl I met on Monday. Tommy and I were down in San Jose, invited onto BayTV's New Media News. The anchor, Suzanne Shaw asked us about the Tamagotchi phenomenon, and about Tommy's personal habits. During our visit we met young Tammie, who was also in the studio. I promised to send her my Tamagotchi as soon as it expires.

A Tale of Two Friends

My friend Tomas's Tamagotchi, Joey, died this weekend. Tomas had taken ill - food poisoning - and in his feverish state he had not noticed that Joey had slipped between his mattress and wall, essentially snuffing out his beeping cries for attention. By morning, with his fever gone, Tomas found Joey. The little bit-mapped baby had turned into an angel, so that it could fly off to Tamagotchi-heaven, or wherever it is deceased Tamagotchi's go when the leave the real world. Tomas seems to have adjusted just fine when I visited with him yesterday. Life goes on.

Aunt Phyllis's Tamagotchi, Dough, has wound up surprising us all. This was the newborn that I was sure would die from overindulgence. But it turns out that Phyllis's mix of overfeeding and low-impact playing spawned a happy mutant: the coveted "Secret Character," whose slovenly lifestyle consists of "Getting up late, going to bed late & is selfish," according to Bandai's Official

Tamagotchi Growth Chart. The character has a big nose and a cap, possibly a beret. He is plainly more interesting to look at than my Tommy, whose simple, appended shape strikes me as boring anymore.

All Creatures, Virtual and Otherwise

The Tamagotchi craze has hatched a whole new category of artificial life forms. The creatures competing for a slice of the virtual pet craze come in two implementations. There are the pocket-able, standalone designs like Bandai's Tamagotchi or Tiger Electronics's Giga Pets (and the newly announced Nano, by Playmates Toys - the first portable pet to feature a human "baby" that grows from infant to child, before it "runs away"). And there are the computer-based, like PF Magic's Petz, Mindscapes Creatures, or Fujitsu Interactive's Fin-Fin, a hybrid dolphin-birdie, in whose underlying artificial intelligence the company has reportedly sunk around $30 million. I keep meaning to delve deeper into all of the above, however Tommy has gobbled enough of my mind-share as it is.

On the truer side of life, my Aqua Babies - Alpha, Beta and Gold - are an absolute joy to own. The spend hours playing a delightful game of tag around the swaying plant (perhaps the bigger guppy is trying to eat the smaller guy?), and they seem to respond to my fingertip when I tap the side of their cube-shaped aquarium. I feed them a toothpick-tip-helping of fish food every other day, and their self-contained undersea environment takes care of the rest. No fuss, no muss. I admire their independence.

Looking Ahead

Tommy just woke up at his usual time, 9 a.m. His age has rolled over to 15 years. He is hungry and bored. I must stop for a moment to tend to his small needs. Three minutes later, he is happy. He ate four helpings of food, and we played six rounds of his silly guessing game, four of which I "won." Once more he is completely happy. For now.

After I file this entry I will resume work on the rewrite of my upcoming novel, *The Deal*. The work is coming along slowly, but steadily. I already know what is going to happen: Sometime in the next few hours, when I am deep into this scene or that, Tommy will cry out for food or attention. I will resent him. But I will take care of him nevertheless. I have no choice. And after each tending-to, I ask myself for the hundredth time: How much longer will this go on?

Week 3

Requiem for a Digital Egg

Tommy died. Bit the digital dust. It happened at 1:06 p.m., just four hours after I had turned in last week's Diary update Week 2: Life Goes On – and On.

It happened very quickly. One minute he was doing his little jig off to one side of my mouse pad, the next he started beeping uncontrollably. The little skull that signals trouble had appeared. Tommy's eyes were tightly shut, his mouth still. He looked like he was sleeping. I pressed the buttons, tried to administer medicine. Nothing. The death process had begun, and there was nothing I could do to stop it.

Eventually the beeping changed its cadence. I think I saw an egg flash on the screen, then a sprinkling of fairy pixels, shifting to the left. Tommy disappeared. In his place, an angel with faintly beating wings. According to the manual, my Tommy had returned to its home planet. (I've read that the Japanese version is more to the point, displaying a gravestone rather than an angel). I pressed the buttons, saw Tommy's final age: 15 virtual years old. The only thing left to do was to reset him and hatch a new bit-wise baby.

53

Passing On

But I did not hatch a new baby (not yet, anyway). I'd promised my purple egg to a young lady I'd met last week. I wanted her to experience the whole process as though the Tamagotchi were brand new. Using a jewelers screwdriver to open the little battery hatch, I reassured myself that it was no longer my Tommy. Just a shell of a life, waiting to begin anew. I replaced the tiny "Pull" tab between the battery and contact, thus snuffing out the toy's tiny spark of life. I packed the Tamagotchi back into its box, stuffed in the manual, and trotted down to the post office to send it on its way to Tammie.

And how did I feel? Frankly, sad. And guilty, for a while anyway. Here I'd just gone on and on about how much I wished Tommy would buy the farm, and then what I'd hoped for happened. Answered prayers. An hour later, I started to miss him. It.

Just a reaction, I told myself. Fifteen days together is a long time. I'd looked after him, nurtured him and, yes, became frustrated by him. I remember my self-assured pride, that because he'd hit the top of the Tamagotchi Growth Chart, that he'd live a long, long life—maybe even a month, I had ventured. Yet he'd only made it to 15, a short life, one the manual rates as "Good job."

On the other hand, Aunt Phyllis's once-portly little Dough has in his eighteenth ("Excellent") year slimmed down to a lithe 3 lbs., 3oz. This was the Tamagotchi I'd all but bet would live a very short life. One of life's little mysteries.

R.I.P.

Feeling a strange obligation to immortalize Tommy's brief life, I checked into one of the Tamagotchi graveyards that have suddenly sprung up—Pullus' Tamagotchi Cemetery. I browsed some of the virtual graves already filled, and read their inscriptions:

A402
CASPER
05/11/97 - 05/17/97
We are very sad that you had
to leave us so soon.

EGGIE
04/26/97 - 05/12/97
my very first chicken and
the very special one
hope you have fun at whichever

I selected a grave in the Water section of the site, filled out Tommy's form, requesting that his inscription read:

TOMMY
05/01/97 - 05/16/97
Thanks for

Another One Bytes the Dust

The next day I received two more Tamagotchi's in the mail, the precious, hard-to-find transparent turquoise model, and the equally in-demand white model. Unable to help myself, I tore into the turquoise one, pulled its little life band, and started the process all over again.

Except this time I vowed to make my new pet live according to my rules, not its own. I fed it when I had the time. Cleaned up after it when I could. Hardly played with it. One night, while off reading in another room, I heard it beeping for my attention. I looked at my clock radio and realized that it was going to sleep and wanted me to turn off its "light."

Instead, I put down the book I was reading and started to laugh. Cackle, really. I am not sure why, exactly, but I thought it was funny. Drew heard me and I told him why I was laughing. He said I sounded like some strung-out hippie mother. That made me laugh even harder. The next morning I checked on the thing and it was fine, sleeping soundly despite the fact that I never turned its lights out.

Eventually, my experiment in laissez-faire parenting yielded a monster. A duck-billed mutant with an ugly snaking tail, doomed, according to the chart, to live a short and annoying life. Six days later, the non-stop beep-beep death knell kicked in, and my second Tamagotchi kicked the bucket. I hit reset again, starting the process for the third time.

Which I've realized is the point. The time. Literally. Since I don't like wearing a wrist watch, the Tamagotchi makes a lovely watch from which my life's single key, to my apartment, also depends.

The Hereafter

I miss Tommy. The real one. Thanks to my time with the virtual Tommy, the real Tommy has moved to the front of my mind. His life was unexpectedly short, too. I've convinced myself that my Tamagotchi experience served a secret purpose. It played an unwitting part in what became a long, drawn out catharsis of sorts. One that will go on for the rest of my life.

It's still a mystery to me why my brother died. I mean, the facts are all there. It was his choice. But what made him do it? What external forces influenced his thought process? Was it the way he was raised by my parents? Then why did the other four of us turn out reasonably well?

Unlike my virtual Tommy, my brother Tommy wasn't just some simple two-bit player. He had hopes and dreams and feelings, the ability to make choices. I wish he hadn't made the final choice he'd made. I wish, like the Tamagotchi, his outside person could re-hatch a fresh inside, a second try to right whatever had pushed his buttons so wrongly, causing him to depart so soon.

So I guess I owe a word of thanks to my digital pet for its small contribution to my life. While others may see it as a simple toy—which it is—it has nevertheless helped me to reconsider some not-so-simple things about life.

Where Tamagotchis go when they've run their random course is beyond my comprehension. As is my brother's final resting place. But thanks to the former, the latter lives on here, in my memory and on the whirring disks that hold this text. For however long they keep going round, so will my version of Tommy.

###

Made in the USA
San Bernardino, CA
02 January 2018